Sky Roads, Sea Roads and Dreams

Rosemary Winderlich

Sky Roads, Sea Roads and Dreams

Sky Roads, Sea Roads and Dreams
ISBN 978 1 76041 868 7
Copyright © text Rosemary Winderlich 2020
Cover: Sama Reid

First published 2020 by
GINNINDERRA PRESS
PO Box 3461 Port Adelaide 5015
www.ginninderrapress.com.au

Contents

Self-analysis	9
There's that pain again	10
Fellowship of travellers	11
First big trip in 1938	12
Thoughts on Independence Day, PNG 1975	13
Wooden Boxes	14
The Unknown	15
Whirlwind in Border country	16
Summer music	18
Airports	19
Lake Samamish, Washington State	20
Arcadia, Nova Scotia	21
On the train to Quebec	22
Online friends	23
Song for Vermont	24
Streams	25
Canyons of New York	26
Give me your tired, your poor	27
Goodbye Vancouver	28
Returning to Australia	29
Filling in the map	30
My new hero	31
A constant presence	32
Early mornings in China	33
Near Lijiang, Yunan	34
Hot morning in Guilin	35
Lazy day at Yaga, PNG	36
Samsam: the new name for Sing Sing	37
Riding the wind	38
Just Landed in Brisbane	39

First arrival in Sumatra	40
Teaching English	41
Farewell to Silangge	42
Pipes	43
Sky roads	44
After my first visit to Angkola country, Sumatra	45
A New World	46
After returning from Sumatra	47
In PNG again…	48
You have been there	49
Between PNG and Sumatra	50
Cloud Traffic	51
Call to prayer	52
Silangge morning	53
Bechak	54
Festival at Damparan Village	55
Leaving Silangge again	56
New layer of memories	57
Three Pagodas Pass, Thailand	58
Dark eyes shining	59
In Kuala Lumpur	60
Halfway home	61
Can Love Hold?	63
To a friend returning from Sumatra	64
Out of step	65
Checking in again	66
Over Borneo	67
Ghost plane	68
Airport Train	69
Photos I didn't take	70
Waiting at Kallang Bugis	71
Steep Stairs	72

Smoke rising	73
There is a valley	74
New child	75
Road untravelled	76
On the road to Sosa	77
Coming in to Jakarta	78
Jakarta night	79
Whispering in	80
Home	81
No more?	82
Dreaming of Siassi	83
Time travel…future loop	84
Moresby Airport	85
Adrift again	86
Mixed emotions	87
Welcome on Tuam Island, PNG	88
Five a.m. at Yaga Village	89
Star dance	90
Empty Terminal	91
Untethered	92
Future grief…or…Silly me!	93
Watching a documentary	94
Return to Sumatra	95
Silangge dawn	96
On the ferry from Samosir Island	97
Google travel	98
Departure Board, Singapore	99
Over India	100
Over the Mediterranean	101
Cathedral at Barjac	102
Die, Southern France	103
Three stones	104

Goodbye to Die	105
Marseille in the morning	106
Midsummer Marseille	107
Old Mahdia, Tunisia	108
Mistral	109
Alchemy in the Medina	110
Melting Pot	111
Rainy night near Mediterranean	112
Changing track	113
Flight magazine	114
Pomerania!	115
Wilderness: watching a documentary	117
Siren Song	118
Morning in Central Jakarta	119
Voice of Indonesia	120
Bangkok streets	121
Just returned from Sumatra…	122
Time telescopes	123
Dreams unfulfilled	124
Change	125
Never More	126
Time's tide	127

Self-analysis
2018

Deep in my heart (more literally, my bowels)
emptiness, a longing for somewhere…where?
Is it the call of laniakia, boundless universe waiting
a touch of eleutharomania – wish to roam free –
or a specific longing to follow a loved story
a phrase, a song, an incident in history?
A story read in *Post* magazine in '44…
cattle drives in the Dargo high country
up the Omeo road, still waiting for me.
or is fernweh just greed, a passion to control –
I want to go there, because I've never been there?

Deliciously intoxicating to let visions roll.
Fernweh is in my soul, semi-domesticated
and I can be realistic, speak sternly to myself
'Retreat! Sleep in my subconscious…
I will dream on a manageable few.'

Fernweh…homesickness for places still unknown
thoughts fly ahead to where my heart waits…

Where am I on the spectrum between wanderlust and fernweh?
…a cup of love of home thrown in, big spoonful of thankfulness
full backpack of treasured experiences, and my memory bank?
Perhaps my mind equates with a cloudy sky…nefelibata…
various formations harmoniously sailing
differing directions, speeds…a glorious skyscape
where one walks alone?

Perhaps fernweh suits best…incurable, I believe.

There's that pain again
2005

An unknown road veers off
my heart longs to follow
but my way rolls ahead…
I'm committed to this track
no turning back.

Roads wide, bituminised
contoured masterfully
or little tracks…
dusty, indefinite
all lead somewhere.

Airports, sea ports people gather
excited preparations
reunions, farewells, departures.
I am greedy to see into their lives
know their destinations

…unreasonable of me
undisciplined I know…
something hides behind the hills
over the horizon, down each track
around the point, over the straits…
up the mountain, or way outback.

I want to go.

Fellowship of travellers
2001

Around the globe
we weave a web of words
across the boundaries
of languages and seas
and friendships grow
In small ways we do our bit
towards world unity.

Your commonplace
my distant mystery…
we travel far to meet
new friends-to-be
share histories
strengthen in small ways
worldwide community.

First big trip in 1938

Leaf shadows moving gently
patterning red-brick floor
a grape arbour
cool retreat behind a shop
room full of bookshelves
sun slanting into darkness…
mellow colours, glowing wood.

Perhaps my deep love for books
leaf shadows and polished wood
the peace they bring to me
began then, when I was two.

Now, as I grow old
my heart yearns for these
and firelight on wood floor…
loves born then, it seems.

Later I reconstructed the story…
fourth baby due
we were sent to Melbourne
big sister six, and I almost two.
Auntie ran a library at Carnegie….
books, dark wooden floors
and leaf shadows.

Thoughts on Independence Day, PNG 1975

Where is my home if this is not home?
I am an alien, but you are my people.
Where shall I go when I must leave you?
Whatever I do, where ever I go
the kundu will beat in my heart
woven into the web of my life
part of my fabric, verse of my song
the beat of the kundu
is one with the beat of my heart.

Be kind to my children
from our land we brought them.
Now this is their home
they have known no other
and when we must go
their hearts will stay here.
This land has shaped them
taught them and loved them…
you are their sister, their brother.

This is your land
I would not claim it
but this land claims me
holds me and owns me.
Sometime we must go
our homeland is waiting
but never
will the beat of the kundu
fade from my heart.

Wooden Boxes

2008

Those little wooden boxes
treasured in memory
convey anticipation
discovery.

They came in the mail
wooden boxes, sliding lids
from the lending library.

My mother chose carefully
stories of other cultures
of countries across the sea
all devoured hungrily.

In New Guinea I taught my children.
…Cuisenaire rods for maths
many colours and lengths, nested
in wooden boxes with sliding lids
dovetailed joints…familiar.

Cleaning up, I found one today
a wooden box with sliding lid…
It once held held sweets, I think.

Wooden boxes, holding explorations
dreams, exotic destinations
lids sliding smoothly in their groves
…beautiful to me.

The Unknown

1998

Places I will never know
experiences untried
vibrate in my mind
always calling me
…exotic to me, but
someone's daily grind.

As I dream
into the unknown
someone
somewhere
is longing to know
this place I take for granted
to explore my here

perhaps
dreaming of escape
from their commonplace
to this far, exotic mystery
very ordinary to me.

Whirlwind in Border country
1964

Whirlwind rustles over the empty street, leaves whisper, fall…
meanders past dilapidated shacks, mine king's mansions
to the silent giant that lies, serrated back scraping pale skies
mounded limbs of mullock, man-sculptured, wind-sanded
desolate, dusty grandeur…
The Fabulous Hill!

Whirlwind meanders on to Umberumberka
over red rock range to Mundi Mundi plain
wide dreaming scribbled scrub of mulga, myall…
on to Mootwingie…sparse, twisted gums
torturous gorges writhing between wind-written walls
dwindling pools gouged in rock-sheathed land
stone slopes, amphitheatres of rock, timeless silence.
Still, bone-still…
only cicadas shrill an endless summer song.

See, high on the still slope he watches…or is it a shadow?
Listen! A faint, far echo of shrill child's laughter!
Hawks wheel in high nothingness
silence vibrates with memory of singing.

…here, on the walls of wind-gouged caves
mouth ochre-filled, they sprayed their hands
drew sacred snake and kangaroo,
on rust-red stone slopes chipped ceremony, history.

Listen!…a voice, patient, flat…
'I wait, white man.
My silent land will drive you out…
fire, drought…
your time will pass, whirlwind in dry grass.
We will return.'

Hot brooding silence listening, listening.
Wind spins on singing a quiet, dry song,
and as night falls, dies.

Mootwingie sleeps.
Mundi Mundi lies dark dreaming
lone myall etched against fire of dying sun
floating over cool emptiness
healing peace of desert night.

Summer music

Wild wheat by the roadside.
random clumps swaying
in quiet valleys
patterns, textures of grasses
varied colours of summer.

They sing to me –
wild wheat, pasture rippling
old, abandoned orchard.

What music do you hear
in summer silence?

Airports
2000

Ghosts of our past…
those New Guinea years
departures, arrivals
meetings, partings.

Three years, then flights south
small plane to Lae
change again at Moresby
children dressed in red
or orange, for easy tracking
drilled in emergency procedures
stay in pairs, hold hands…
what to do when lost…
name, et cetera, around each neck.

Once the boys' suitcase was mislaid
we learnt a hard lesson.
From then each carried a small bag
books, pencils, a change of clothes
water bottle, toiletries.

For me, an exciting time…
anticipation, urgency, promise.

I enjoy airports.

Lake Samamish, Washington State
1999

There, on the map…intriguing, unfamiliar
enticing me for days…Lake Samamish
but on my explorations around Seattle
I went other ways.

Today I walked the long way round
to get a glimpse of you, Lake Samamish.
Arching maple trees, afternoon sun low
tall, dark pines of Indian lands
between them a glimpse of Samamish…
perhaps birch bark canoe near distant shore
perhaps smoke rising from hidden lodges
or only mist?

My path left water's edge
turned up dim Waowona forest
vernal, primaeval, listening silences
an Indian behind each tree, observing me…
delicious frisson of fear
thin veil between then and now
billowing curtain, door ajar.

Up a slope, and suddenly
back into my century…
a fallow field, murmur of cars.
Indians retreat into the gloom.

Goodbye, Lake Samamish.

Arcadia, Nova Scotia

Realising dreams is tricky stuff.
Will the reality deflate the fantasy?
Dreams sweetly matured, aged in time
absorb different flavours, assume character
perhaps different from the original.

Here walked Longfellow's Evangeline
and Gabriel, her beloved…
rudely torn from their new roots in Grande Pre
outrage still remembered by Quebec students
…web of deceit, driven from France
then expelled again, from their Arcadia
by the English. Many eventually returned
not to that rich, hard-won tidal valley
to poor, coastal land, as fishermen.

Evangeline and Gabriel separated
never gathered again with family
briefly reunited only on his deathbed.
Sad page of history, dimmed by time
truth and reality twisted together…
Longfellow's saga is largely fiction.

I wept over them in childhood, and again here
watching the tide lap at these embankments.

What an achievement, harnessing that tidal bore.

On the train to Quebec

Larches pierce the low hills of Nova Scotia
rugged country of marshes and inlets
cranberry bogs and low, stony ranges
lupins and phlox wild by the rails.
Late afternoon, sun sinking
larches islanded in still dark water
soft draping firs, birches, long-legged
dancing in slanted evening light…Arcadia.

Shallow stream curving around stones
sky wide angel blue, pale to the horizon
strataed clouds dark above.
Gaspe Peninsula, Notre Dame Mountains
north over wide bay, sunset's glory
still estuary of the Restigouche
pale pearl waters of Chaleur Bay.

Gaspe lies dark, distant bagpipes calling
mist rising over darkening sea
murmuring pines, moss-bearded hemlocks
pristine as when the Huguenots came
fleeing from France, seeking a new home
as when Gabriel and Evangeline walked
in the forest primaeval, their Arcady
'where sea fogs pitched their tents
among mists from the mighty Atlantic'.*

---

* from *Evangeline*, by Henry Wadsworth Longfellow

Online friends

As I travel on, it's good to know
at my next stop waits a friend
as yet unmet
except on the internet.

I know her name, her interests
her age, career and habitat.
When my day's journey ends
we meet as friends.

Not a superficial passing through
a tourist's view
but warmth of home and family
a glimpse into community.

My new friends generously
share time and dreams
so when I leave I carry part
of each place in my heart.

Song for Vermont

I'm leaving the woods of Vermont
Mad River rushing down its canyons
Camel's Hump bold on the skyline
hummingbirds and mourning doves
nuthatches chirping, chickadees scrape
white wooden houses, lush meadows
swift-running rapids…I'm leaving.

Thank you, Vermont
for soaking me soft in green summer days.
I've walked your forests, climbed hill's summit
looked down on Mad River's tempestuous flow
scent of pine trees, birdsong resounding
made memories to share as I go.

Here they struggled through pristine forests
Deer Slayer, Hawk Eye, heroes of Fenimore Cooper
here the trek north of captives to Indian homelands
tales I read often throughout childhood…
Now I have seen where those stories were set.

Train rockets towards Massachusetts
green country morning fresh.
Goodbye, verdant Vermont
long anticipated, so soon behind me.

Streams

Vermont's Mad River scrambles, irrepressible
over long, laughing distances, carving its way
squeezes through gorges, reckless, unpredictable
into the Winooski, then wide Lake Champlain.

Broad St Lawrence, grand, majestic
rolling unstoppable on to the sea
carving the land through time and flooding
dividing nations, shaping history.

My heart answers small streams
springs bubbling from hillside
eager brooks over pebbles rejoicing
laughing on their tumultuous ride
down rapids of rock, chasms of stone
at last into flat land, maturing, settling
youth over, pace slowing
still travelling on.

Canyons of New York

Pink moon sinks down canyoned street
sky rectangular between towering buildings
smoke from Canada's fires misting the north.

Times Square, humanity shoulder to shoulder
languages, sweat, debris in dark corners
patient police horses stately and tall.

Many screens flashing, assailing senses
various levels and configurations
changing messages flicker and shine

and high over this compressed humanity
pink skies and smoky orange moon
announce Canada's tragedy.

Give me your tired, your poor

Sea splashes on the feet of Liberty
rolls on and is gone
melds into the ocean, returns
with more battered humanity
caring nothing
the implacable, levelling sea.

I sought forebears' names
searched through boat lists.
Alas, they entered at Halifax.
I was there days ago
and didn't know.

Frantic ants swarm busily
round the feet of Liberty
rush, pass on, and forget.
The statue stands.

Thousands left their lands
and found, at journey's end
liberty?

Hopefully, eventually.

Goodbye Vancouver

My first foreign city, except New Guinea.
I walked streets, shops, visited prisons
sailed around the harbour in an Umiak
explored First Nations sites.

University, summer holidays
wide avenues of spreading trees
halls of learning echo, empty
basking in sunshine by the sea
First Nations totem poles
bold against the sky.

Such a small glimpse of this land
soaring mountains, rolling prairie
rivers tumbling to the sea.
Canada, I'd love to know you.
Vancouver, I'd love to stay
but I must go home today.

Mountains cool against evening sky
dark islands floating in pearl sea
then we are over cloud
and away.

Returning to Australia

Glowing warm cocoon
hums through endless night
sailing relentlessly on
an enclosed world
on to Australian summer
golden fields of dry grass
rounded hills, rounded trees.

Behind me, brooding pines
steep hills, deep lakes
majestic, blue and green
Sibelius scenery!

Australia…muted earth colours
olive, grey green, dust
tawny shades of tan and rust
beautiful to me
endless treasures to explore.

Torn again…
my heart is slow returning
from a distant shore.

Filling in the map

Strange names on the map
intrigue me
tease me
questions rise

When I have travelled there
the map lives
songs sung
voices, birds' cries.

I have coloured in small areas
of USA and Canada
…satisfaction.

Now there are known faces there
new friendships growing
fewer blank spaces.

Home again I leaf through
maps in my mind
satisfied
for a while.

My new hero
2009

Leafing through a magazine, the word Huguenots leapt out at me.
I am sensitised to this word through Longfellow's poetry,
Evangeline, about the Arcadians, of Nova Scotia
refugees from France, forced from home again.

Matthew Fontaine Maury, a Huguenot, joined the navy in 1825.
Frustrated by haphazard instruction he set out enthusiastically
using cannonballs to practise spherical geometry…
puzzled over what I call 'sea roads', pale pathways on the sea
marking mysterious currents, or formations deep below.
Rounding dangerous Cape Horn, Maury was shocked
at lack of information on winds and currents there
meticulously recorded his experiences
later published *The Navigation of Cape Horn*.

From 1839, retired, he wrote articles pressing for reform
demanding higher standards, ethically and educationally
a naval academy teaching mathematics, chronometry
international and maritime law, and natural history.
He was a leader in meteorology, oceanography, hydrography
instituted a worldwide system to share maritime information.
…a story to inspire a poet? Well, he interests me.
but he was not popular for exposing inefficiency .

Looking out to sea from our small island in PNG
pale roadways winding on still sea fascinated me.
Maury's enthusiasm to learn, his Huguenot origins
his interest in those sea roads, resonates with me.

A constant presence

I feel you, Siassi…
mountains high across the sea
a steady presence in my life
humming insistently…
blue and green symphony.

My Bali Hai…floating high
a world away, long years away
but still I clearly see
waves rolling in unceasingly
high aisles of palm
cold, pristine streams
clustered palm huts
and around smoking fires
faces dear to me.

My cloud-crowned island
always present deep within
I am rich because I know you.

Siassi
you are part of me

Early mornings in China

Walking backwards in mist
beside veiled Suzhou lake
four Chinese women
struggling to communicate
laughing at my efforts.

Isolated in dim cloud world
I walked backwards with them
four laughing Chinese women
and me, in crisp morning air.

In Shanghai's park
misted morning patched
with exercising groups.
Graceful t'ai chi teams
echo ancient patterns.

Wet country morning…
farm door frames rain falling
on ruined castle, wide fields.
No t'ai chi today.

Mornings, Shangjhai, Beijing, Guilin
I crept out early in search of a park
t'ai chi, boot scooters, line dancers
folk dancing, fan dancing, walking
laughing…welcoming.

Near Lijiang, Yunan

Yunan hillside
tall, graceful bamboos
arch overhead.

Misty mountains of Yunan
rice terraces shining.golden
stairs to the clouds.

Early morning
sweepers sing up the cobbled street
brooms over shoulders.

Minority groups
in colourful costumes
thread down to market.

Evening. Paper boats
bear candles and prayers
down dark stream.

Hot morning in Guilin

Mist rising from slow water
soft plop of fish jumping
rooster call echoes from far hills.
Fisherman poles bamboo raft
rattles oar to call cormorants
black heads rise to silver surface.

Swaying bamboos frame silent river
sunlight clothes the stream
iridescent butterflies around our feet
shot silk in blue and green
leaf falls from rain tree, spiralling slow
mist rises from the water.

Heat grows as day invades
farmers pass on their way to market
tour boats follow the deep channel
on towards Yangshuo.
We sit in shallows, out in the stream
under umbrellas, and wave.

Bamboos whispering
kharst hills reflected in quiet water
fisherman black against silver…

hot morning in Guilin.

Lazy day at Yaga, PNG

Sea strataed blue on blue, clouds piled high and white
slim areca palms against the sky, over forty feet high
move sedately side to side…each with its own rhythm
fronds furling, unfurling in stately pride.

A grove of coconuts, fronds longer, lighter
ripple in syncopation, each a different beat
as waves rise and fall in sky ocean
echoing unseen streams of air, respond
to invisible currents somewhere up there.

Tall palms dissect sea's pale horizon
sway sedately in different directions
inward curling, then unfurling
teased by breeze, patterns ever changing.

New Britain always watching
silent across the straits.

Samsam: the new name for Sing Sing

Shrill singing rises up the night…
some find it discordant.
I hear with heart and memory
it is melodious to me
a unique harmony.

You view my video
perhaps are amused to see
people decked in branches
feathers, dog's teeth, leaves…
I hear through grateful tears
music embedded by years
beautiful to me.

Depth and meaning of that life
community woven, tied
by those voices
rattle of palms, sigh of sea
smell of aromatic leaves…
music indivisible from these
woven into my fabric
precious to me.

Riding the wind

All checked in and waiting again
state of suspension like a dream
look deep in the eyes of each dear friend
one last wave from the door of the plane.

Long months of planning, looking ahead
anticipation of meetings, laughter, tears
thoughts of that island filling in my mind
…now far behind, all far behind.

Flight Moresby to Cairns, quickly done
now whispering in, whispering in
gliding, sliding, riding the wind
back to Australia again
time in New Guinea like a dream
whispering in, whispering in
vibrant life, sweet community
over and gone into history.

So here I live on, there they live on
so long the distance in between
still love and pain our lives entwine
I in their hearts and they in mine
so any day though far away
I feel their love flow through my life
slipping, sliding sweetly between
tasks and troubles and time apart
spanning distance, reaching to me
whispering in, whispering in
touching my spirit with love again.

Just Landed in Brisbane

A world
a world away
from those wide seas
islands palm crowned
shining white sand
a world, a world away.

Just in from Moresby
bemused
confused
melancholy
so far, so far
from Siassi.

A life, a life away
sweet community
surf's slow song
sea breeze
rattling palm trees.

This life holds me
inescapably
with tasks and blessings
so here I must be
so far, so far from Siassi.

First arrival in Sumatra

2005

Medan's teeming suburbs past
we rise from the plains to Siantar city
reflections of the Dutch, grand mansions
then Parapat, Toba dreaming white
hot ginseng coffee by the lake
camaraderie of late-night travellers.

On…deep ravines, narrow bridges
through Lambun Julu, bamboo-plumed
winding up and over to Porsea
church spires and elaborate graves
then Balige city on Toba's shore
Batak rooflines piercing the sky.

Dark pines march with the winding road
twining down, around then up
to Siborongborong, Sipaholan
surreal chalk cliffs, hot water springs.

Left at the crossroads, past Tarutung
steam rising along mountain edge.

Warm world rolls through the night
radio's glow…Batak songs rising, falling…
I wake again to high mountain pass
pines thrusting from deep ravines
moonlight, mist, then down to Pahae.
Not long now to Sidimpuan.

Teaching English

Faces turned to me
listening, listening
doubts, frowns…
swift clouds across the sun
then understanding dawns
eyes shine.

Significant event
suspenseful film?
No…
phonetic symbols
a secret code
valuable tool.

They seize the concept
hungry for words
exultantly attack, analyse
words words words
reduce them to symbols
and pronounce them
unaided.

Doors opening
mysteries revealed.

Farewell to Silangge
2005

Those special days
those months
of love and singing
grieving together
those magical days are gone.
Time moves on
those days a warm memory
hold them soft and easy in your heart…
smile remembering.

Soon I'll be gone far, so far
I pray you will understand
my heart is there with you.
My heart is there.

Memories are there to build on
to hold when you are cold…
there are better things ahead.
Look back in love
and forward trusting God.

With Jesus in our hearts
we are always together.

Pipes

Pibroch of Donnuil Dhu
calling down the misty glens
bone and fibre of the clansmen
twining through their days.

Pipes of Ireland…pipes of Peru
in many lands the pipes are calling
speaking to the hearts that hear them
embedded in their dreams.

Bamboo pipes of Sumatra
Batak pipes, Angkola pipes
twisting, knitting voice and drum
calling down the clouded mountains
weaving into my heart.

Sky roads
2005

I travel sky roads home
while yours winds back
through lush valleys
rugged mountains
down, down to Pahae.

Dark hills, wide valleys
rice fields shining
steam rising along the mountains
crowding villages, noisy markets…
Sumatra!

Evening
still hours to go
flutes call from hill villages
from gatherings around fires
twisting, tangling up the night.

Road now dear to me…
my heart follows you
while my sky road leads home
flutes weaving in my dreams.

After my first visit to Angkola country, Sumatra

2005

I hold it warm within me
a flood of gratefulness
new joy and pain
new love glowing
stirring in my heart.
You cannot see
this is now part of me
a painful growing.

I try to explain
but you were not there
to hear and feel and see
and the visions in my mind
don't quite come through.

I hold it gently in wonderment
swelling love and thankfulness
this part of me that's new
a glory and pain
now always with me.

Words are inadequate
but I will try
to share my heart with you.

A New World

A world, a world, a world away-
a world I never knew
contours of land and lake and hills
ridged rice fields climbing steep slopes…
Sumatra, I never knew you.

A wealth, a wealth of song
complex, rich harmonies
strange beats, metres, intervals
pipes skirling, weaving in between
a treasure trove
never imagined.

A world, a wealth
I never imagined
blank map now three-dimensional
contoured with hills
roads curving, rivers flowing
faces, places now dear to me.

So poor
so poor I was
before I knew you
Sumatra.

After returning from Sumatra

2005

(Texting new to me!)

I am at peace.
Although it's night
the skies are blue…
I've heard from you!

Long silence broken
my mobile to yours has spoken
and you replied!

We've found a way
through clouds
of distance and confusion
and communicated!

Now everything's all right
heart at peace
hope again has woken…
I've heard from you.

Ties are not forever cut
though so far, so far apart
your mobile to mine has spoken!

In PNG again…
2006

Hot, bare Moresby
then over the mountains
steep green valleys
mighty, winding Markham
smoke rising from villages…
and down to Nadzab.

Heavy, humid air hits
as that first time…
four bewildered small children
me in durable nylon dress
never worn again in PNG.

Here you are again, to meet me.

We are all older, slower
thirty years have passed.
Hearts slip into sync
minds align, eyes speak
loves and losses tie us together…
gentle cords, but strong.

Long night to Siassi
rolling, surging through the night.

How could I stay away so long?

You have been there

And did you see
above Finschhafen
as you drove up to the seminary
Umboi island rising high above the sea
cloud crowned, majestic
breathlessly beautiful to me?

Did you hear
on the islands of Siassi
drums, singing rising through the night
far chanting through thick, tangible moonlight
sea rolling, rolling in with quiet might?

Did you watch
wall of water advancing
heavy rain marching, roaring
towards the island over the sea
closer, closer…then obliteration
nothing visible of our wide mission station
but children dancing, dim, through the rain?

Between PNG and Sumatra

My iPod waits, full of Indonesian
to soak in as I drive, work, walk
but I don't want to let go
of these past weeks in my island home
of words, songs in Saveng and Mbula
sweet to my ears, my mouth.

My plan… March, pack away iPod
to give my slow brain time
to dredge up Saveng and Mbula
from deep in my subconscious
Reluctantly I put away Indonesian
sweet to my mouth, my ears
soaked in Siassi songs and phrases.

Now, leaving Siassi again
lifted on sea and song and love
surf slap, slap on shore
wind singing in from New Britain…
grieving leaving these islands and seas
wild drums, palm trees…

May already… My iPod waits
to immerse me in Indonesian, which I love
but my heart holds these others, which I love
ties shared, lives so dear, so near
involuntarily my mouth forms, tastes phrases…

My iPod waits to reprogram my brain.
…perhaps tomorrow.

Cloud Traffic

Cloud fleets
orderly ranks sail east
shadows follow
small islands look up and see
feathered foreign entity.

I look down and see
a life unknown to me.

White furrowed fields
strataed ridged snow hills
one moves implacably south
one floats sedately east
some same direction
different speeds
as curved sea roads
ordered by mysterious forces
echoing undersea terrain
paint pale paths on calm sea…

Beyond sky range, clear blue
stretches to high cloud castles
snow plains glide, slide
in currents around their feet.

Slim streamers of dark cloud ahead…
rain in Jakarta.

Call to prayer

First one for me this year
I heard in Singapore
in Arab Street.
In Medan they skirl and skein
twining, climbing
defining otherness.

In Siantar, surrounded by mosques
call to prayer wakes me suddenly
weaving into the fabric of life
into memories.

In Sidimpuan
through the night
they twist into my dreams…
essence of Indonesia.

Early morning, six or seven
different voices and styles
rising smoke, fluttering veils
cutting through traffic's roar
meandering upwards
interlacing, wandering
stitching the sky
as the faithful honour their god.

Silangge morning

2007

First morning
across the valley chakchaks* call
somewhere out of sight
clouds mist far mountain view
majestic and beautiful
gentle breeze stirs cocoa bushes
new leaves tender pink

Downhill the kampong wakes
bustle and noise
here high on Silangge hill
calm and still.

Each year, the excitement of return
entering crowded Sidimpuan
meeting friends
then familiar road north to Sipirok
even the potholes dear to me
winding up the surrounding hills
where this precious world waits.

Left off the highway
up the narrow stony street
I am here.

* chakchaks: black and white monkeys

Bechak

Definitely not well sprung…
potholes recorded in my bones
well ventilated, rain friendly
exhilarating
close to the earth in a bechak
at face level with walkers
at one with the crowd.

Two-stroke motor put-putting…
this old motorbike has seen life
now ends up here
capsule attached
pottering around town
…economical transport.

Bechak travel is an experience…
embrace it.
Lordly tourist buses roar past
towering, isolated.

I am among the people.

Festival at Damparan Village

Day of rejoicing
now late, still we gather
unwilling to end the celebration.

Smell of smoke…fire, crack, spit
dim lamplight flickers, gleams
catches eyes, smiles.

Sleepily heaped together on mats
singing, singing
laughter and voices intermingling
dimming, rekindling
sharing stories
pipes skirling.

Heaven will be like this.

Threads, filaments twining
knitting memories
through smoke-scented sleep.

Leaving Silangge again
2008

Interesting, looking back…
older children graduated and left
after years as family
balance shifting, sliding.
Those left moved up a notch
some willingly, some sadly
longing for those leaving
then my goodbyes to the sad remnant
and a long bus ride.

Time stretches, deadens, edges fray
my sudoku book is finished
shampoo, toothpaste dwindle.
Long wait in Jakarta airport
again in Changi
threads stretching, breaking.
Sudden separations are painful
this way – dwindling, dwindling –
is perhaps easier.

Another plane, fighting up
three times removed from you
and my heart is heavy.
I am far from there
and not yet anywhere.

Later I will tell the happy stories.

New layer of memories

Singing and dancing around fires
at ceremonies and festivals
warmly gathered in community…
or travelling through the night
with Batak songs on the radio…
music now embedded in me.

Batak people weep as they sing
music now alive to me
with faces, senses, places.
Years ago I might have disliked it
now it carries memories.

Back in Australia I play tapes
sing along with loved songs
weep for children left behind
once again…
for dark pines arching the road
friends travelling along with me
Batak music playing.

Three Pagodas Pass, Thailand
2009

From Bangkok we drive up the valley to Sangkhlaburi
past the bridge on the River Kwai.
Centuries ago the Burmese army came this way
invading unsuspecting Thailand
marching down to Bangkok with elephants and pageantry.

Higher up, into the mountains
to beautiful Lake Vajiralongkorn, actually a reservoir
spire of submerged Wat Sampasob piercing smooth surface
close against Wang Kha island, where Mon people live.

Sangkhlaburi waits, strung above the lake
panoramic views, fresh mountain air.
In the streets, in traditional costumes
minority groups, refugees from violence
in Burma – Myanmar now –
no rights to education or medical care.

Secret communities hide in the jungle
children attend illegal schools far from town
each evening creep back over the border
watching for Burmese soldiers.

Hiigher up, Three Pagodas Pass.
Armed guards stand at the border
boomgates bar the Burma railway
built by prisoners of war in the 1940s.

I walked closer. Guards raised their guns.
It didn't look very different on the other side.

Dark eyes shining

They came secretly to the border to meet us
smiling children from a Burmese orphanage.
A slim girl in the back looked into my eyes.
Without words we communicated.

The children left us
to creep back into Burmese territory
where their parents had been killed
where they are unwelcome
threatened with death.

Smiling girl
you are in my heart.
Your photo watches from my piano
as I pass your eyes look into mine.

Dark-eyed girl
orphaned, life full of uncertainty
eyes clear and calm, smiling at me
Where are you now?

In Kuala Lumpur

Sari's glowing, Tamil language flowing
spice-scented night.
India broods over the horizon
out of sight.

From Australia
I feel New Guinea far north
breathing, drums calling…
Waltio, lewa blong mi
mi sori long yu…I long for you
I thank God I walked with you.

Sumatra, beating in my heart
di dalam hatiku
deep my love for you
weaving of Batak music, land
and language enfolds me.
Teman teman, saudaraku, pahompuku
rindu, rindu…I miss you.

Over the horizon your lives flow on
mine flows on here
my heart full of gratefulness.

Halfway home

On the screen the plane creeps closer
further from my second life
closer, closer to my home.

What do I feel as I draw nearer
nearer to family and friends
other friends fade further, further
other life grows distant, distant…

confusion, sadness and suspension
losses as I look behind me
also hope as I look forwards
planning, reassessing. changing
to be more useful in God's garden
living more effectively
in my Australian family

Prayers, and hopes are crowding, glowing
though my heart is sad and lonely
friends unmet, mistakes unmended
in that life quickly receding
faces dear in dreams appearing
faces behind me and before me.

This my burden and my blessing
past and future intermingling
as I float far above Australia
suspended over the Red Centre
mind and heart confused and waiting…
further, further from Sumatra
slowly, slowly nearing home

Nothing in this life is free
I am paying for my blessings
in a no man's land suspended
as the plane drifts ever closer
returning to familiar places

and yes
the gifts are worth the rending
again my Lord will lead me through
dislocation and heart mending
growing into someone new.
He has things for me to do.

Can Love Hold?

Can love hold strong so far
so far?
Time flows.
Will love remain
withstand the strain?

Wait for me
keep heart space for me.
If God allows
I will come again.

To a friend returning from Sumatra

You were there…
curving round pine-covered hills
Lake Toba sleeping white
Samosir dreaming…
my heart rises as I remember
Batak country claiming me.
speaking to deep within me.
Did it vibrate in your heart?

If I had lived another life
it would be Batak…
my heart Batak.

Perhaps if Australia was denied me
far and worlds away
I would yearn for all things Australian
…long road from Ceduna
wide wheat fields, spreading gums
deserts of red soil and stone
night sky wide dreaming
perhaps. I can't explain…
the Batak land is in my heart
wide screen forever unwinding
behind my daily life here
music ever welling up…

Batakness has soaked into me.

Out of step

I have returned
Sumatra far behind me
and here I am
home, and out of step.
I left
widened life and view
but still I care for you.

Home again, I want to fit
into old friendships.
Some, perhaps, can see
part of my heart is far away.
I long to pick up threads
but no longer quite belong
in the same way.
I have moved on.

My heart is stretched
that other world now part of me
so I am not quite here, nor there
out of step and lonely.

That world is dear
I won't, can't cast it off and so, I guess
I'll always be a little out of step.

Checking in again
2014

Check in
discard
excess baggage
thin down
luggage
through Security
no alarms!

Check
ticket
bag
phone?
Check
passport
coat
Indonesian currency?

All done.

Hold on
underneath
the everlasting arms…
soar free.

Over Borneo

2014

Sprawled lights below
I'm flying over Borneo
Kalimantan now
in my mind
Borneo, wild land of mystery
near the octopus, Celebes (now Sulawesi)
drawn in geography classes…
names tasted, rolled over my tongue.

Ion Idriess, *Forty Fathoms Deep*
read and reread in childhood
pearl divers from Koepang and Malakka.
Of course I searched the atlas
hungry to know these places, fascinating, far
spice wars, intrigue, massacres on these seas
greed for nutmeg, cinnamon, cloves…
these islands waited, silent in my subconscious.

More recently, children of Indonesian workers
no identity, no education, no medical care
also a charming, erudite lecturer from Sabah
I met in Adelaide years ago…
and orangutans, of course
an unknown nation tantalising me.

Flickers of light in the darkness
snaking glow of fires as I pass high over…
I saw you, I felt you there below, Borneo.

Ghost plane
2014

Roaring on through cloud
Jakarta to Singapore
coast of Sumatra receding.

Below, pale river delta
reaching towards Pekanbaru
Riau under our wings.

Cloud plains stretch forever.
Gentle rock, bump of air pockets
unseen currents playing with our plane
descending to Singapore

and perhaps we cross their path
perhaps they passed this way
unknowing, reading, dozing
or in growing panic
knowing something was wrong.

Their spirits sail forever into history
vanishing into misty cloud plains
the region of dreams.

I pray pain was brief, end sudden
the greater burden left to families
carrying their pain and loss
through long years of grieving
and not knowing.

Airport Train

Packed tightly
teenagers plugged in
matrons dozing
some, as I, analysing
imagining histories
unobtrusively, I hope.
Happiness of young couples
eyes speaking, currents arcing
tourists loudly declaiming
all the faults of Singapore
experts, just off the plane.

Me, just off the plane
half asleep, slow to orientate
followed a kind businessman
He found me studying a map.
This way, he said.
This way, smiling
three changes of trains
then our paths diverged
he first checking
that I knew my way…
courtesy personified.

Lives intertwining for a distance
then spinning off in different orbits

that brief thread remains
part of my weaving.

Photos I didn't take

This is me, actually in Singapore
strolling past Raffles hotel
in my kung fu pants, PNG bilum
colourful Indonesian shirt
wispy hair too short to tie tidily
lush palms, manicured lawns
and me, definitely not manicured.

This is me, in Raffles…almost.
Long waiting list, strict dress code
watchful doormen.
But here, in Raffles bakery
almost Raffles
sipping Raffles special blend coffee
pale and bland
nibbling a Black Forest concoction
rich and luscious.

Raffles
epitome of colonial luxury
shut to me.
Through the window
pristine white settings
attentive waiters
elegant diners.

I was there…almost.

Waiting at Kallang Bugis

Business opens at 12
so I wait.
Friendly café next door
tasty coffee
carrot cake on my plate
I wait.

Out of the way corner
of busy Singapore
residential it seems
freestanding two-legged tower
surrounded by green
far from anywhere
I wait.

People pass purposefully
destinations obviously known.

I drink coffee
wait patiently.

Steep Stairs

Chinatown, steep stairs
dark wood, hollowed by years.
This is how they lived
immigrants around the world
escaping to Shangri La, Eldorado
and a new struggle.
Now – millionaires, skyscrapers.

Steep stairs long escalators
into the bowels of the earth
under Singapore streets
down to Little India Station
a twinge of claustrophobia…
so far up to the light.

Steep stairs in backpackers hostel.
My back has known its share of stairs
backpack heavier with years
my time in places like this ending
…too steep for me.

Steep steps down from the plane
to noisy Medan tarmac
heat and bustling throng
Hello again, Polonia.

Sumatra, I am back again.

Smoke rising

Childhood
dancing around clearing fires
burning off stubble
friendly fragrance from winter fireplace
frightening on dry summer days
bushfires looming.

Moresby past, over the dark ranges
down to wide Markham
smoke rising through palms
misting blue mountains
a prayer, a whisper, welcoming me.

Riau, smoke always rising
symbol of mourning, jungle dying
oil palm encroaching
animals wandering bewildered…
old paths, inborn memories
disrupted. Unfriendly smoke.

Around pale lake, Sumatran plateau
down to Pahae Nauli. Smoke rising
from gardens, kampongs
speaking of families, memories
drowsy murmurs around the fire
smells of cooking
friendly smoke threading through my life.

There is a valley

There is a valley there
golden with rice between dark hills
small towns with cobbled streets
white, steepled churches.

The people there
are courteous and loving
villages jewel winding roads
through the wide golden valley
the beautiful Sipirok valley.

There, on Silangge hill
my heart is tied
selengleleng nae
there children I love
work and play.
There is music and laughter.

I long to be there.
Sipirok and Silangge…
words that mean nothing to you
are words of love
written in my heart.

New child

New child arrives…abrupt energy
brimming with self-confidence.
A few days and she grows into my heart.

Potentiality, insatiable desire to learn
to grasp knowledge, hold the world.
Eyes fix on mine, widen, shine
thoughts spin deep, assessing
mouth moving involuntarily
each word tasting, caressing
eyes echoing wonder awakening
wonder of communication
understanding flowering in her eyes.
Now wedged in, grown in to my heart
I can't imagine time before
this strong, free spirit touched my own.

Far away she grows on without me.
I long to see her emerging personality
respond to her endless why?
and sliding through each day I see
her smile of joy, eyes shining into mine
sharing wonder with me.

Now it dawns on me: dark-eyed girl
you are the spirit of my childhood
intoxicated by this world's wonders
greedy to know, to go, to see.

Road untravelled

New road leading to where I have never been
blank spot on the map, where I have not stood
each bend opens a new vista
perhaps not so different from many others
but somewhere I have never been.

Bulamario passed, Batu Satail far ahead
steep path away, a jungle track.
Marancar close, but we turn another way
to this raw, jagged valley, steam rising
spurting from fissures by the path
seeping between stones beneath our feet
moonscape, chaos of earthquake, and landslide
sulphur smell.

Picnic over, we wait, warm, relaxed
time suspended in this steamy valley
between Marancar and Bulamario
high above Sibolga, to the west
far Pahae mountains to the north.

Our bus comes at last.
We wind down, down
from this high land of steam and aren trees.

Another unique piece of this world seen.

On the road to Sosa

Gentle morning light
softens hard edges
mountains fade into haze.

Down, down into mist
fresh morning light
air cool and kind.

Later harsh sun
will reveal ravaged land
now veiled from sight.

As the sun rises
ethereal mist become smoke
from clearing fires.

but now…a fairy land
suspended in golden cloud
as we wind down to Riau.

Coming in to Jakarta

Almost there.
Down through grey haze
veiled shapes
oil tankers perhaps
or rusted barges
clothed in smoke.

Below, misted harbour
lace chiffon draped
translucent, pale
far down, down
scribbled lines
muted brown scallops
on still sea
fanning, curving out
pale pastel tracery
delicate brown lace
…garbage, I think
perhaps sewage on the sea
distant, misted from here, above.

We float in quiet and serene
city below seems gentle, clean.

Jakarta night

Deep night
and still the roar
the tide below
traffic's never ending flow
sound softened by height.

Constant traffic
echoing the stars…
candles float in dark stream
dark, dreaming stream
and I, alone up high
dream down.

How many are alone
down there
in the ceaseless stream
hiding behind smiles
caught in their lonely dream
as I dream down
from my balcony.

Whispering in

Long night over, roarings cease
I wake again to warmth and peace
whispering in, whispering in
sliding between clouds satin smooth
soft slipping between, slipping between
layer on layer of silken fleece.

We rose with a roar, roared through night
leaving Asia's colour and heat
on, on until far to the east
horizon glowed with a dim red light.
Now sun shines and all is still.
Over cloud fields we quietly sail.

Below in smoke and traffic's roar
life waits to engulf me once more
but for a time I am warm and still
glowing cloud fields beneath the wings
whispering in, whispering in
engine grasps air, wheels click in place
loves and losses fall far behind
and in the roar the future sings.

Down from the shining white cloud plain
slipping between, sliding down between
looking up now to a ceiling of grey
winter landscape green below
and already new dreams and visions flame
built on the riches I have gained.

Home

Home
homecoming
going home…
but home is behind me
heart drawn and quartered.

Home is family
but what family…
what is family, my family?
I have many families…
places I have lived, loved
each owns a part of me.

Goodbye, sisters, brothers
of my heart, not blood
I leave you far behind me.
Hello again, Australia

Poised on the the edge, the cusp
balanced precariously between.
Past slides into my subconscious
treasured, stored apart.

Old life zooms in…
another new start.

No more?
2015

Money is short. Obligations grow
For ten years I've spent mid year there
this year I cannot go

and will I ever go again
to where the pine-clad mountains rise
highway winds through crowded markets
rice fields shining by the road,
steepled churches along that high plateau
past Tarutung and down to Pahae below
then up the old volcano's rim
through smoking Aek Latong
where my heart rises…
almost home.

Many memories rest on Silanngge hill
children, laughing, singing as they work.
or sharing fear and hurt.
There is so much I have gained…
I have grown and learned with you
and thank my God for all He's given me.

No more?
No more to sing with you, my children
no more to hear your voices?

So much I will miss
but countless riches in my heart.

Dreaming of Siassi

Lying here awake
thinking of friends old and new
of future meetings
with those who walked with me
in my mind's eye, my heart I see
crowds waiting on the jetty
hear the shouting, climb ashore
immerse in the rejoicing throng
noise, heat, laughter and song
scent of leaves worn.
Dark faces shine
tears in your eyes and mine
rattling palms, sea breeze
dear familiar melodies
such joy to be there once more.

Dozing, I smile, weep sweet tears
to meet again after many years.
My Lord, you are so good to me
please let it be so, let it be so…
give me strength to once more go
to pray with them, reminisce
thank them for their goodness to us
be with them on that dear shore.
once more.

Time travel…future loop

My heart leaps on ahead
things done, words said
conversation, work and play
I smile, laugh, revel in it all.
Then come goodbyes.
I grieve. Tears fall
though
I'm still at home
nowhere near leaving…

and so my thoughts roll on
scenes unfold, buds form
stories blossom from dreams.
I taste, feel our time together
each laugh, each sigh
the love, the pain.

I sit sad, hollow
missing that life, missing you
sharp pain of separation
sad long months that follow.

The present fades away.
These days I dream may never be
but they are real to me.

Now is the time to book
Air Asia fares are low.
Late June I'll go.

Moresby Airport

2017

Waiting, hours to spare.
studying people, interactions, et cetera
Speakers blare, Goroka boarding.
Calling all passengers
Passengers for Wau, Buka, Alatau
Lae, Madang, Lorengau.
Signs in Motu, Neo-melanesian
…strange words.

Passenger lounge thronging
various heights, bone structures
faces strained, bored, impatient
or smiling in anticipation.
Some peaceful, confident
some serious, focusing inwards
a funeral party, dressed in white
mine workers returning from leave
file aboard their flight.

Where they go someone is waiting
…colleagues, parents, family.
Unknown to you all, my story.

We pass…a glance, a thought
perhaps eyes meeting
lives briefly intersecting.
An airport unlike any other
and like every other.

Adrift again

Adrift…
friends far behind me, more ahead.
Here, just me, uncertain, free
no destination but north
escaping winter's aches and pains.
…an island afloat, a drifting boat.

Not always comfortable
uncertainty, instability
no role, no recognition
so this is how new arrivals feel
our forebears long ago
and refugees now…
untethered, suspended
longing for community.

People pass on the street
some smile, but don't know me.
A little lonely, I long to see
the soul of this community
be one with them…but here
I have no role, no years to spend

Can't have it all…freedom
and also a place in community.
My present choice…to wander free.
Too soon I will be anchored in one location.

Mixed emotions

Travelling north in PNG
towards my old home
cloud crowned Islands in the sea…
twelve hours on the ship to reunion.

Threshold between two worlds
Australia behind me
old loves coming closer
while a few hours further north
the bleak world of refugees
grief and pain imposed in our name…
islands of horror and shame
just a few hours further north.

Mixed emotions…
thankfulness in returning
and heart sick at inhumanity…
rejoicing and mourning
struggling together
as I near sweet reunions.

Northwards again to love.
further north over heaving sea
desolation, oppression.

When will they see loved ones again?

Welcome on Tuam Island, PNG

2012

We near…
shore bursts clear
gathered crowd
tapestry of sound
tambourines, drums beating
blended voices enfolding.

We follow
up ridged island spine
a singing group on each step
and behind all
drums insistent beating
sea washing on the sand
and joyful greetings
glorious cacophony
twining sound all around

Others have joys I cannot know
but mine, mine
this glorious, embracing
enclosing, heart-warming
sea of sound
carried by rhythm of drums
permeating recesses of my mind

treasures to mine.

Five a.m. at Yaga Village

I wake to a vibration, something calling
almost unheard, but dear. It calls me
but my bones have 40 years more wear
and though I yearn to follow I stay here
listening to rise and fall of chanting voices
as sea sighs in.

Distant singing, rattle of palm trees
chanting voices caress my ears from far
where they wait to see the morning star
announce time to cease dancing…
Saparikrik sings.
So many nights like this in my store
drums woven with sea's quiet voice
drums slowing as Biri rises high.

Silent figures beneath dark trees
silhouetted against pale seas
going to wash in Wara Jaga.
Bell rings…a gentle touch
to wake cooks but not delegates
sleeping in the village above.

All sounds dim here, down by the sea
boats tug, waves slap, light slowly grows.
New Britain emerges from piled clouds
morning life begins
…and Lord, I thank you so much
that I could come back again.

Star dance
2017

Farewells and tears past
long, strong embraces…
sorrow and death between us
and next meeting.

Siassi low behind us now
under heaped dark clouds
island fading, sky darkening.
Tuam to our left, misted, dim
Malai low to the right.
We head out for Finschhafen.

Deepening darkness
the ship thrusts on
surging, checking, rolling.

Darker, darker…
horizon fades, then gone
only white lace of our wake
and stars dancing…
Cross lying low to the sea
Belt of Orion rising, falling.

Ship's rail bounds dim world
darkness all around
stars, swaying, dancing
travel with us

Empty Terminal

Late arrival from PNG
waiting early morning departure

I search for a corner to doze.
Offices, counters shut down
coffee shops one by one close
empty echoing space
distant hum of technology
beast breathing unseen.

Travellers waiting early flights
as I am, wander aimlessly.
I settle down on a padded bench
hidden behind a doughnut stall
feet on suitcase, bag under head
for security.

No sleep at all…
random passers-by all night
distant clang of cleaners
echoing out of sight
hum of vacuuming.

Morning comes slowly.

Untethered

Back in Adelaide
drifting untethered…
Up there, community
now only me.
Gone, rain trees' shade
dusty potholed streets
and friends.

Which way now?
No signs visible
floating
no tide, no current.

Sori long yu, Yaga nambis
sori long yu, olman meri
sori long yu, Wara Varanda
mi lusim yu longwe, longwe…
sori long yu, wara Tarawe
sori long yu,
Pasis Malangon
long skies away
long seas away

between again…
nowhere for a while.

The wound will mend
treasured scar remain.

Future grief...or...Silly me!

I go knowing
I will grieve leaving.
I leave grieving
go to love
arrive in joy
but deep within
still grieving
though now
in happy reunion
already
I see ahead
to leaving.

How many ways
how many ways
can one heart grieve
divide in pain
heal, reach out again
swelling with love
accepting future grieving
with thanksgiving?

Watching a documentary

Kyrgyzstan…so far, so far away
where your memories are centred
years of tears and praise invested
I feel your pain, your joy.

Stark mountains strong against the sky
cold streams tumbling down
into beautiful Lake Issy Kul
I imagine you watching, yearning…
familiar languages, loved faces.

I understand to some extent
longing in my heart for a far island
mountains rising blue to stormy sky
endless seas encircling
islets spray-misted, palm-crowned
and I know you feel for me.

Dear friends live on there
loved voices calling on that shore
where we invested heart and years
love and tears.

Your understanding comforts me.

Return to Sumatra

2018

Sumatra, I am coming
engine humming, thrusting on
through the window, smoke and mist
far below, the wrinkling sea.

Sumatra, plane descending
coming closer. Now I see
over the island clouds are piled
veiling mountains dear to me.

Polonia airport, hot and crowded
gateway to my other land
thump of wheels hitting the tarmac.
Land dear to me, I have returned.

Sumatra – love and music
many streams and misted mountains
loving friends and celebrations.
I am here.

Silangge dawn

Morning star bright
dark bamboo plumes
palms silhouetted
rooflines angular
stark against the sky
thick mist billowing.

Rooster crows down the village
smoke rises, saucepans rattle
fog rolls up the cobbled street.

Cold morning on Silangge hill
misty figures drift to wash
morning star fades into light
bamboo plumes now green.

I hear the rolling, grinding
as morning sambals are prepared
return to the warm kitchen…
smiling faces, glowing fire.

On the ferry from Samosir Island

Suspended in time, mind slows
distance flows
slipping, sliding.

Batak music pleads on the radio
engine throbs
Samosir fades.

Bemused by gentle rhythm
the day slows
quiet time flows.

Ship's rhythm transports me
to New Guinea seas
long years ago

behind us Samosir grows smaller…
not far to go.

Around the headland, Parapat
steepled church against the hills.
Medan road waits.

Google travel

I planned to visit Europe
Frequent Flyer points enough
friends and relations to see

maps of significant areas
connected with our family tree
studied, exhaustively
but then I volunteered
was sent to Sumatra…
now embedded there.

Points, credits, money spent
on returning, returning
to my Angkola family
Europe, sadly, necessarily
now not a possibility.

I am content, usually
and grateful I was sent
to that land now dear to me.
Almost satisfied…

Now, unexpectedly
continuing on from Indonesia
surprisingly, unbelievably
I am on my way to France.

Departure Board, Singapore

Idly checking departure time
and…is that Mandalay?

Mandalay!
loved, exotic name
childhood visions
rich bass voice singing
'On the road to Mandalay
where the old flotilla lay…
Burmese girl waiting…'

My bowels stir again.
I'd blocked out possibilities
little money or time
body ageing, slowing
packed away long dreams
now
one word…
my armour ruptures

Burma comes sailing out full blown
into my conscious mind again.

Over India

Over Kandahar
a little north of Karachi
vast arid ranges
endless expanse of sand

the world too wide
to fit into my time
my life, my mind
…but my shadow
the plane's shadow
perhaps
brushed some place below
perhaps
I passed directly over
striped the sand…
perhaps
someone looked up
saw my plane's plume

and wondered.

Over the Mediterranean

Sumatra ten hours behind me
below, the Mediterranean.
Quinquireme of Nineveh sailed majestically there
Romans besieged Carthage, where Dido reigned
ships hurried towards Troy to reclaim Helen
and the Heroes rowed forever, on their long quest.

Wide brown Nile still empties into the blue sea
familiar shapes: Italy the boot, known from maps.
I see nothing…aisle seat, bulkhead, shades down
our dim world roaring on towards Frankfurt.

Soon perhaps Meteoria will pass below
feel the shadow of our wings, then Venice.

I have consciously narrowed my horizons
curbed my wanderlust, no longer plan to see all.
Susan waits in Marseille, country cottage booked
one corner of Southern France, an unexpected gift
three weeks exploring little towns and rural life.
This will do, I thought, this little taste of Europe
but time soaking in ancient history
stacked stone cottages from 11th century
angular alleyways, balconies, fan-paved streets
walking on centuries of blood, love, tragedies
peering down winding lanes into other lives…

My sensibly suppressed desires to go everywhere
are in danger of breaking out again.

Cathedral at Barjac

Silent stones
soaked in years of worship and tears
sins confessed
centuries of hymns sung with devotion.

Vaulted dome thronging with prayers
scent of incense lingers
stone steps rounded by centuries
of penitent knees
silence vibrating with souls long gone.

Wood panelling, carvings of saints…
and who sat each evening in this pew
Sundays, saint's days?

Carved Jesus on the wall
reminder of the price he paid
His great love for us.

Dim cathedral still, so still
air alive with currents
dreams, agonies, hopes.

Saints, impassive, look down.

Die, Southern France*

Bare, stark cliffs hide the sky
guard the Drome valley

Between chestnut trees
dusty, narrow lanes
squat, square gatehouses
of long-lost estates
some broken, bare
occupied by squatters.

Hot summer haze
wheat fields in the sun
sparse shade of sighing pines.

Old men walk slow
a woman invited me to sit
we laughed and gestured
I learned a little French…
only Indonesian emerges.

Down shaded lanes new vistas glimpsed
corners where lives are lived
doors open to the street
below curved balconies, window boxes

and always the mountains watch.

* Die is pronounced Dee.

Three stones

Stones shining in the River Drome
sparkling, glowing in the stream.

Summer day in southern France
lazing by the river
mesmerised by water flowing
twisting, parting, joining
smooth, seamless entity
flowing on through history

stones
sculpted by melting snow
various textures in my hands.
I chose three small ones
brought them home.

They sit on my windowsill
dry, plain, still
…add the magic ingredient
and they will glow for me
take me back to River Drome
singing over shining stones
near Die.

Goodbye to Die

We leave out haven by the river
wind up the street for a last croissant.

Faces just becoming known
a waiter from our café hurries past
a family we met a few days ago
a couple from our camp wave
and there, those grand Leyonberger dogs
I have conversed with twice.

Just beginning to feel at home
but we must go.

Winding around the mountain's feet
high crags frowning down
over the bridge, Drome flowing below.
Westward next towards Vallens
clinging to mountain's edge
twining channels plaiting, skeining
water sparkling over stones.

Medieval village, ruined castle
then the mountains fall behind
river curves away northwards
we turn south towards Marseille.

Goodbye, Die.
Goodbye, River Drome.

Marseille in the morning

Cool breeze blowing over the bay
to us high up the hill
Later hot and crowded
now Marseille is spring cool.

Industrial yards, machines, cars
usual train line scape of outer cities
graffitied walls, derelict towers
busy highways, barren cement cuttings
now a long dark tunnel…
perhaps an underground railway?

We pass a hillside village…
crags and ruins, a castle of course.

The road sweeps around to the bay.

My heart turns back to the streets of Die
ancient buildings, cobbled lanes
slow life, relaxed community.

Perhaps the old city of Marseille
will satisfy me.

Midsummer Marseille

Noon
windows shuttered…all sleep.
Hot, dusty, dry
rather like Australia…
little exotic French character.

Down by the marina, sea breeze.
We wandered towards the train station
climbed the hill, siesta still
and found character!

Angular lanes, mysterious doors
pressed, wrought or beaten iron
wooden doors, studded, carved
narrow gateways secretive
each unique.

When doors open
shops, cafés emerge
businesses behind the doors
carving, grinding, sawing
creation and community
behind each unique door
in the cobbled lanes
of old Marseille.

Old Mahdia, Tunisia

Sea slapping
engine softly chugging.

Steep stairs in old Mahdia
inlaid with tile fragments
from Carthaginian times
climb to trellised rooftop café
haven from hot white glare.

We drink our tea
watch changing sea.
Sunlight floods cubed houses
shadows lengthen
sea pales, sky pales
wind gently rattles palms.

Reclining on padded seats
sea breeze blowing
we drink sweet mint tea
with almonds and pine nuts
to music of George Wassouf.

Shadows rise up the walls
mellow gold paints rooflines
limns boats in the harbour.

Sun sets over the Mediterranean.

Mistral

Breezy morning
Mistral blowing
dust gusts
shirts flap
hats escape.

Carthaginian mansions
tall rooms, cool and still
thick stone walls
wrought-iron rails
marbled steps winding up
to rooftop gardens.

Steps subtly patterned
cream and grey
edges thinned by years
arches
vistas to a far courtyard
and another
and another
fountains murmuring.

In the streets
hot, dusty wind
all in motion.

Here inside, quiet and cool.

Alchemy in the Medina

Flasks voluptuous line the walls
shining gold and jewel hues
Ange au Demon, Lavender
Bleu de Chanel and Rose Amore
mysterious ingredients
gathered in from sun-drenched fields
from dark forests, tropic shores
travelling far
to the hidden back room here

where magicians blend perfumes
distilled from flowers, bark and spice
in their alchemy transformed
into essences and oils
shining golden on these shelves
in the Medina of Tunis…
Angel, Poison, Fahrenheit
Nina Ricci, Violette
Mimosa, Hypnose de Lancome
Code Lunar and Opium.

Through the realms of alchemy
family secrets, chemistry
now gathered in this little room
glowing walls of bottles bloom…
Kunza, Diesel, Allure d'homme
Jasmine Noi and Music Blanc
Borgeous, Santal, Fifth Avenue
Pamplemousse, La Coste, Lulu.

Melting Pot

Hurried, worried, preoccupied
some seem angry, arrogant
many friendly, welcoming.

At first, sameness, a blur
but soon differences emerge
faces swim up from the crowd
slim, elegant, sensitive
smiling, serious or proud
threads woven from history
Africa, Morocco, Phoenicia
and France, close across the sea
a similar blend bears evidence
of long interaction.

Fair, reddened by sun
or dark, lean, long
African crinkled hair
dreadlocks, blondes
great variety here.
Jewish migrations
Moorish occupation
seafarers of ages
faces all shades of dark
evidence of antiquity.

Time…our senses develop
we see individuals…
the beautiful people of Tunisia.

Rainy night near Mediterranean

Through the night rain falls down
caressing earth and sea and town
and in the sound I hear the pain
of conflicts past, and then again
the silent roar of passing years
conflicts, separations, tears.

I feel the chill and misery
of homeless people on the sea
the hopelessness, helplessness
of bewildered, fleeing refugees.

Through the night rain falls down
gently on land and sea and town
and in the sound is comfort's song
for families gathered safe at home
blotting out sad voices of the lost
struggling, hunted, tempest tossed
the loneliness, the emptiness
of the battered and bereaved
their pain of separation from
a homeland they must leave.

Lord, bring them to a friendly shore
where they can live in peace once more
beneath their own roof, safe and warm
sheltered at last from life's fierce storm
listening to a friendly rain
blessing their own roof again.

Changing track

Engine changes, starts to slow
reel in dreams, change pace
and so I must change track
prerequisite to coming back.
I must land, sometime, somewhere
can't stay forever in the air.

Over Adelaide we swing
wheels click into their space.
I try to turn my mind around
detach from that loved place.
Below the clouds the future waits.

A gift…this time to reassess
measured new analysis.
I must break free, discard excess.
Each time the same: too much.
To travel light seems unattainable.
Strategic planning: multipurpose
muslin cloth as scarf, skirt, sheet
but here I am, much the same
juggling bags, trolleys and back pain.

Resolutions: lighten mind's load
simplicity, freedom, flexibility
but beware! Take care!
Possessions accumulate
responsibilities proliferate
habits grow tentacles, procreate.

As I wait to board another flight
I plan disentanglement.
Next time I'll get it right.

Flight magazine

Delicious visions, vistas unknown
meant to tempt, of course, and do
limpid water, beach pristine…
Lombok, I think.
Pulau Sampurna, lagoon cool blue.
Near Malang, Java. Meteoria
rising primaeval from Greek plains
and Ambon – spice wars, intrigue –
now a peaceful tourist destination
picturesque bay, wars far behind.

Returning after months away
I had fixed my thoughts on home
reeled in ever flowing dreams
to concentrate on practicalities
tasks awaiting me – gardening
spending time with family –
but I opened the flight magazine
and new dreams streamed in.

I am returning, reunions wait
not the time to plan ahead.
I resolutely shut the magazine
comfort myself with what has been
hoard of memories stored
gifts received and vistas seen
try to concentrate on now.

Pomerania!

So where do I fit in this wide world ?

First recorded ancestor on Dad's side of the family
listed on the roll of Danish knights, a Dane.
But no. Recent discovery: that Danish knight
came from Pomerania, therefore my new fascination.
Hmmm, let's Google Pomerania...
Archaeological traces through Stone and Bronze Ages
Iron Age. In the middle ages, Slavic tribes and Vikings
established homes and dynasties there.

About AD 1000 Poland invaded Germany
the area became Pomerania, land of the sea.
In the 14th century, the remaining Wends
or Kashugians and Slovincians moved east.
What a saga! Perhaps I will test my DNA...but
how can tests possibly unravel such complexities?

Pomerania, a land of antiquity
new to me, except for those little dogs
so Germanic and Slavic...now Pomeranian!
Aha...perhaps I share the Vandal blood
I envied in my children, from their father's side.

How could Ancestry tests possibly sort out
the original elements of my genealogy?
Stir in new herbs now and then, stew a little longer
wars, dispersal...start again
some elements of each era holding on tenaciously?

Imagine, loyalties stretched this way and that
previous relationships forbidden, buried
as powerful nations conquered, partitioned
imposed their wills, purified ethnically?
Imagine the dislocation, loss of identity…
necessary deceptions, hiding traditional loyalty
denying family?
But whatever my genes, I am just me.

Now the Wends…descendants of Slavic Gypsies
also known as Vandals
as 'Huns, Vandals and Goths' who pillaged Europe.
Google says Berlin was originally Wendish, or Sorbish
then the Wends settled in eastern Germany
my husband's grandmother a Lusitanian Wend
so my children are part Vandal…fascinating!
Each human is a complex web of interactions
many varieties, threads, interconnections.

Wendish forebears came to Australia from the Spreewald
a land of waterways, where Wends had retreated
and in Australia, they added threads to the tapestry…
my mother's mother was Polish, her father German.

Borders moved with each war
perhaps Grandfather's DNA was Polish…he looked Polish.

So interesting, those lives lived long ago.

Wilderness: watching a documentary

The wilderness is calling me
voice deep and strong and wild
across Russia's endlessness
myriad landscapes, animals, trees
and never ending pines
her heart-filling immensity
fills me with awe
Across the Bering straits, Canada
same depths of white, frozen woods
man insignificant in pristine snow
soul of the land humming deep.

Sibelius' deliberate, deep symphonies
were made of these vistas grand…
nature's cathedral, pillars to the sky
silence profound…wilderness!

I have breathed my share of this world's beauty
but if there could be, somewhere
a corner of wilderness for me
to stand among trees, wade in clean streams
live in simplicity
with wind and rain and seasons turning…

My mind is drawn inexorably
into the music of that land
drawn unresisting into endlessness
air clean and pure, woods limitless…
wilderness.

Siren Song

Long frond
slow unfurling banner of dreams
wind harp fluting high
minor key yearning
strumming my heartstrings…
sweet slow chords diminishing
gone

bereft silence
banner unravelled, song silent…

still dreams seep into my sleep
roads untravelled unravelling singing.
I long, heart twisting
to retrace each song to its source.

Another one yearning in…
who comes home
from far unknown?
What have they seen?

Another and another
no rest to settle, forget.
Flight path above
siren song seducing me
planes fluting in, dreaming in.

Morning in Central Jakarta
2019

I step out onto my tiny balcony
traffic's roar, acrid air flood in.
Below, streets and buildings at angles
skyscrapers looming through haze
manicured gardens round their feet
rusted hovels hugging their boundaries
and somewhere a rooster crows.

Here on floor 27 giants look down on me
an exclusive, proud family
reaching 40, 50 floors into dull skies
traffic roars, roars, miasma rises
through the smoke the call to prayer rises
sirens scream desperately seeking
and the rooster calls.

Down, down, down between tall buildings
thronging canyons of cement and steel
down, down from my tiny balcony
cars, motorbikes crowding, speeding.

Far left a wide expanse of cemetery
directly below, tidy rows of chillies grow
and still the rooster crows.

Voice of Indonesia

Evening. Here's the call again
from high buildings all around
one dominant voice, others distant
meandering, spiralling song
twisting upwards
piercing the smog
fingering around tall buildings
weaving a veil of devotion
and memory
following ancient patterns
circling up through the haze
scribbling, spinning
twisting into random threads
blending, flowing.

Early morning, noon and evening
the three knit into one thread
a minor harmony rising to their God.
I pray with them, over the busy city
from my balcony.

He hears us all.

Bangkok streets

Open a new door
slip sideways
a different story
unfamiliar…
touching other lives
invisibly transforming
perhaps some resistance…

change will come
can't be prevented.

Faces in the street
moulded by ancestry
many ancestries
difficult to analyse
though I like to try.

Each imprints on me
something, some fragment
rupturing preconceptions
my future diverted slightly.

I am changed.

Just returned from Sumatra: driving through central Australia

2018

Wide sweeps of dry country
beauty in wind sculpted tree
groves of stunted gums, tea tree
grey, olive green, pale blue
underlaid by red earth…
a subtle tapestry

time to think…

Loves just left, far behind me…
I try to rationalise, loosen ties
reconnect with life ahead
left months ago
resurrect connections
rediscover planned directions

where from here?

A time of healing, rolling south
fitting my life back into place
processing grief, regret.
So much unfinished there
and also here.

I know there is a task for me
and I am blessed with love and memories
each time more in my heart's store.

Time telescopes

In my heart the waves roll in
on those dear shores of Siassi
seasons of living, dying, pass
but in my heart time telescopes.
Those days are always close to me
those seas roll in my memory.

Dark Sumatran forests roll
draped on mountains wild and steep
emerald rice fields round their feet.
Long history lies on this land…
rajahs in hill fortresses
warriors on sturdy ponies ride
weapons tipped with datura
storming high wooden palisades…
and always pipes and drums.
Time telescopes…it is now.

Childhood memories are sweet
roaming our Riverina farm
riding to school, a magical way
purple pea flowers, martin's nests…
seventy years ago, or more
that time is part of me today.

Down the tunnel of long years
these memories glow steadily
those times flow on with me
have made me who I am
so long ago…but here and now
they live on in my memory.

Dreams unfulfilled

I might never go
up the grey-green, greasy waters
of the Limpopo.
I will never see
Popocatepetl in her majesty
Chimborazo, Cotopaxi shimmer in the sun
high condors over the Andes sweeping
silent snow-capped mountains sleeping
wide Zambesi run.

But I have seen
New Britain's smoking mountains rise
like Bali Hai in turbulent skies
couched lions in wide Chinese field of rice
sentinels of glories past
Guilinn's slow river flow between bamboos
and distinctive hills of karst
ageless Ubirr singing over flood plains
unending high, sky roads
Borobudur brooding dark.

There are many places I will never go
a thousand mountain tracks call, 'Follow me'
untried country lanes whispers 'Come and see!'
tug my heart. Loved places draw me back
but Chimborazo, Cotapaxi
Shangri La, Karakumy over the horizon glow
forever veiled in mystery.

Change

Time winding down, drawing in, narrowing
days fade away

road once stretching to ininfiity, reels in
diminishing

all retreating, backing into the core
thin into mist.

My road will grow again in other ways
these changing days

my store of memories will stay with me
to comfort me

though they must relax their hold on me
so I can see

as they reel in, new roads are leading out
framed differently.

Times change and I must readjust to fit
or atrophy.

Never More

Settling delicately in my heart
permeating every part
seeping from mind gently weeping
throat tightening, bowels longing
…never…never.

Unbelief heavy in my mind.
Can this be possible – never?
I asked my Lord for direction
Go again, stop now, or when?
Am I too old to go?
Is it unreasonable to think
I can still be useful
in that far corner of Indonesia?
Might I be a liability?

so much love, received, invested
how can I stay away
how explain to the children?

An emptiness…if never
where can I fix my dreaming
essential to my existence.

Lord, I pray I can accept
…but never?

Time's tide

I can hear the time approaching when I can drive no more
when I cannot follow side roads that entice me to explore
when my eyes or mind or muscles do not let me qualify
to be master of my movements on sea or road or sky.
I can hear time's tide approaching with a steady, quiet roar
flooding down dry riverbed with a slow relentless bore
trees bending in the distance as the winds of time blow free
distant heavy rain approaching like a wall across the sea.

So I long to be away now on the wide road travelling
or overseas to places dear to meet friends there again
rest my eyes on vistas significant to me
where I have lived and laughed and loved, places of memory.
Spread before me vast, wide landscapes created by your hands
let me wander long, clear beaches, barefoot in the sand
paddle in fresh, stony creeks, crest hills, absorb new views
feast my eyes on Australia's palette, satisfying earthy hues
venture to places new and far to know my country more
so when at last I'm grounded and travelling is done
I can relive past adventures, walk again each distant shore
roam in my mind's garden, reopen every door.

When at last I must stop driving, my time of travelling cease
let me relinquish independence with humility and peace
trust you to lead me onwards, overcome regret and fear
to follow new directions which I know you will make clear.
And I thank you, and I praise you for all you've given me
always there to guide and comfort, always travelling with me.

www.ingramcontent.com/pod-product-compliance
Lightning Source LLC
Chambersburg PA
CBHW070918080526
44589CB00013B/1349